MILITARY

Diane Lindsey Reeves

Created and produced by
Bright Futures Press, Cary, North Carolina
www.brightfuturespress.com

Published by
Cherry Lake Publishing, Ann Arbor, Michigan
www.cherrylakepublishing.com

Photo Credits: cover, Shutterstock/Oleg Zabielin; page 5, Shutterstock/Aleksashka; page 5, Shutterstock/ Vaclav Volrad; page 5, Shutterstock/isuaneye; page 7, Shutterstock/aarrows; page 8, Shutterstock/Natykach Natalia; page 9, Shutterstock/Jirsak; page 9, Shutterstock/anders photo; page 9, Shutterstock/Soulart; page 11, Shutterstock/Balefire; page 13, Shutterstock/Greg K_ca; page 13, Shutterstock/Chris Bradshaw; page 15, Shutterstock/Charles F McCarthy; page 17, Shutterstock/Pavel Chagochkin; page 17, Shutterstock/givaga; page 19, Shutterstock/Konstantin L; page 21 Shutterstock/Cheryl Casey; page 21, U.S. Marine Corps; page 23, Shutterstock/iurii; page 25, Shutterstock/Thanapun; page 25, Shutterstock/Eugene Sergeev; page 27, Shutterstock/Vormin Beeld; page 29, Shutterstock/Rafal Olkis; page 29, Digital Storm.

Library of Congress Cataloging-in-Publication Data

Names: Reeves, Diane Lindsey, 1959- author.
Title: Choose your own career adventure in the military / Diane Lindsey
    Reeves.
Description: Ann Arbor, Michigan : Cherry Lake Publishing, [2016] | Series:
    Choose your own career adventure | Includes bibliographical references and
    index.
Identifiers: LCCN 2016020221| ISBN 9781634719124 (hardcover) | ISBN
    9781634719353 (pdf) | ISBN 9781634719582 (pbk.) | ISBN 9781634719810
    (ebook)
Subjects: LCSH: United States--Armed Forces--Vocational guidance--Juvenile
    literature.
Classification: LCC UB147 .R45 2016 | DDC 355.0023/73--dc23
LC record available at https://lccn.loc.gov/2016020221

Printed in the United States of America.

MILITARY

There are five branches of the United States military.

The Air Force. The Army. The Coast Guard. The Marines. The Navy.

Each branch keeps the peace in different ways. The Air Force provides air and space power, mostly with planes, helicopters, and satellites. The Army provides land power. When there is a threat to peace, the Army movies into a troubled area to secure it, and restore it to order before leaving. The Coast Guard protects waterways in this country through daring rescues, law enforcement, and drug prevention duties. The Marine Corps is a "rapid-reaction force." When a conflict begins, Marines are usually the first "boots on the ground." The Navy's job is to secure and protect the oceans around the world. During peace time they keep the seas safe for travel and trade.

Land, air, or sea? In the trenches or behind a desk? Close to home or overseas? Where would you like to serve? Read on to explore your opportunities in the military.

TABLE OF CONTENTS

AIR FORCE PILOT

Air Force officer with both eyes on the sky needed to fly sleek fighter jets or "heavies" used to move cargo and troops and to fuel jets in mid-air. Must have perfect eyesight, excellent motor coordination, and ability to safely operate very complex machinery. Cool, calm, and collected response to stress required. Willingness to travel overseas on a minute's notice especially appreciated.

- **Ready to take on this challenge?**
  Turn to page 6.

- **Want to explore a career as an Army Cyber Officer instead?**
  Go to page 9.

- **Rather consider other choices?**
  Return to page 4.

Find out how things fly at **http://howthingsfly. si.edu**.

Up, Up, and Away!

You are sitting in the cockpit of an **F-22 Raptor** fighter jet waiting for clearance to take off. You are an Air Force **pilot** assigned to the Air Force Weapons School at Nellis Air Force Base in Nevada. Your job is to train the trainers who teach elite pilots to fly one of the most advanced fighter aircraft in the world. It goes without saying that you are one of the best pilots the Air Force has to offer.

The F-22s are known for speed and **stealth**. They can travel at twice the speed of sound and are hard to spot on radar. They can be flown night or day in all types of weather at altitudes of up to 65,000 feet (19,812 meters). This fighter is armed with heat-seeking missiles, radar-guided missiles, and radar-guided bombs. F-22 Rapors can perform both air-to-air and air-to-ground missions. In other words, you do not want to mess with this jet anytime or anywhere.

Top Gun Training

The only crew aboard this very expensive aircraft is you—a well-trained pilot. Your training began as a cadet at the U.S. Air Force Academy in Colorado Springs, Colorado. After graduating as an Air Force officer, it was on to flight training, assignments in this country and overseas, more training, and lots of time in the air.

Now, years later, you are taking your place on the runway and getting ready to lead a flight test **sortie** of four F-22s. The other pilots are instructors you have spent months training. They are tough, well-prepared, and totally focused on the mission at hand—just like you. That's a good thing since you will be flying at speeds of more than 1,000 miles (1,609 kilometers) per hour in tight **formation**. One false move and you are toast.

As flight commander, you aim for a completely successful mission. Your team has poured over flight plans and practiced on **flight simulators**. You all know what to expect from beginning to end. You have also prepared for many emergency situations—just in case. Throughout the flight your radio commands will guide your **wingman** and the other pilots through every maneuver.

You are confident that your students are ready to train combat mission-ready pilots to fly the world's most powerful—and expensive—fighter jets. You have the right stuff! Now it's time to prove it.

Your Air Force Pilot Career Adventure Starts Here

EXPLORE IT!

Use your Internet research skills to find more about the following:

Orville and Wilbur Wright and their first flight

The history of aviation

Famous pilots like Amelia Earhart, Charles Lindbergh, and Bessie Coleman

TRY IT!

Name That Jet

Pilots know their planes. You can get acquainted with common types of commercial airplanes by keeping your eyes on the sky. See if you can identify a Boeing 737, a Boeing 747, a DC9, and an Airbus 330. Hooked? Find out all you can about different types of jets and keep a journal with notes about the ones you spot in the sky or at airports.

Paper Flight

Make a fleet of paper airplanes and conduct your own test flights. You'll find instructions at www.foldnfly.com. Experiment with ways to balance the four forces necessary for flight: drag, gravity, thrust, and lift.

ARMY CYBER OFFICER

Patriotic computer nerd needed to protect Army networks and systems from cyberattacks. Technology skills must be superb. Ability to outsmart hackers and other online menaces a must. Strong leadership qualities needed to guide and inspire tech-savvy cyber mission teams. Top secret security clearance required.

- *Ready to take on this challenge?*
  Turn to page 10.

- *Want to explore a career as a Coast Guard Rescue Swimmer instead?*
  Go to page 13.

- *Rather consider other choices?*
  Return to page 4.

Be a "website warrior" at **www.nsteens.org/ Games/WebsiteWarrior**.

Cyber War

You are a high-ranking Army **cyber officer**. Disciplined. Decisive. A well-trained leader ready to fight your nation's battles. Your battlefield? Cyberspace. Your weapons of choice? High-tech computers. Cyber enemies, beware!

You are assigned to the brand-new Cyber Protection Brigade in Fort Gordon, Georgia. This elite unit didn't even exist a few years ago. There was no need for it before. The bad news is that cyberattacks are considered one of the top threats to national security. The good news is that technology, the Internet, and cloud computing have brought new opportunities for gaining the upper hand with terrorists and other enemies of peace.

Problem-Solving Starts Here

You are in charge of several teams of technology whizzes who use impressive computer skills in both **offensive** and **defensive** ways. That means they start and stop problems. For instance, one of your teams recently used technology to "turn out the lights" in a foreign military zone. This offensive action gave cover to a team of military **commandos** who used night vision goggles to drive out a nest of **terrorists**. The blackout, plus the element of surprise, helped these **boots on the ground** in a faraway country. The commandos were able to fulfill their mission without endangering innocent civilians also living in the area. This type of offensive tactic is one way your cyber teams support combat missions.

Another team under your command sits in a cluster of desks equipped with computers and lots of monitors. They take defensive actions to protect the military from cyberattacks launched by hostile opponents. For instance, when a cyberspace **espionage ring** tried to break into the Army computer network to steal defense secrets, your team stopped them in their tracks. There will be times when the enemy successfully breaks into defense systems, but your team is ready to react quickly to minimize the damage. **Malicious** cyber activity doesn't stand a chance against your team!

Not on My Watch

Both offensive and defensive actions take a lot of training, problem-solving, and practice. It's your job to make sure your cyber warriors are ready to do battle in operations around the world—while sitting behind desks and working in cyberspace.

Your Army Cyber Officer Career Adventure Starts Here

EXPLORE IT!

Use your Internet research skills to answer the following questions:

What is a hacker?

What is malware?

What is a cyberattack?

TRY IT!

Cyber Security Starts Now

What can you find out about how to stay safe online? Make a poster with at least five tips to share with classmates or ask your teacher if you can do a presentation about cyber safety to a younger grade.

Computer Whiz Kid

Cyber officers represent the best of the best when it comes to computer skills. It's not too early for you to get a jump start on your cyber training. Take a first crack at computer programming using free online resources like Scratch (https://scratch.mit.edu), Code Academy (www.codecademy.com), and Hackety Hack (www.hackety.com).

COAST GUARD RESCUE SWIMMER

Comfortable being tossed around in 10 to 20 feet (3 to 6 meter) waves? Able to think and perform challenging tasks while underwater? Ready to swim the distance as a Coast Guard **rescue swimmer**? Ideal candidate can handle hard core physical and mental training. Bring a deep respect for the sea and willingness to help save lives under dangerous conditions.

- *Ready to take on this challenge?*
  Turn to page 14.

- *Want to explore a career as a Deputy Secretary of Defense instead?*
  Go to page 17.

- *Rather consider other choices?*
  Return to page 4.

Sink or swim with these water safety tips at **http://bit.ly/StationSafewater**.

"Mayday, Mayday, Mayday!"

You are a certified **rescue swimmer** stationed at the Coast Guard Air Station Kodiak in Alaska and have spent your entire life preparing to respond to distress calls like this.

It started at the neighborhood swim club when you were a kid. In high school, you were captain of the swim team. You had a swim scholarship all the way through college. You decided to join the Coast Guard after you saw a show on TV about how rescue swimmers saved thousands of people stranded in flooded areas after **Hurricane Katrina** caused levees to break in New Orleans, Louisiana.

The training was tough. You had to master 11 ways to approach, carry, and release a survivor. You had to complete 8 different water rescue exercises. And you had to pass a grueling physical training exam by doing 100 push-ups in two minutes, 100 sit-ups in two minutes, and 19 pull-ups. But, hurray, you did it!

To the Rescue

When the distress call comes in, you are on duty aboard a Coast Guard **cutter** off the coast of Anchorage in the Pacific Ocean. A fishing boat has capsized and five fishermen are adrift in a lifeboat. They will all die if you do not get there in time.

You spring into action, grab your gear, and climb aboard the **Dolphin helicopter** waiting on the top deck. You are soon in the air on the way to rescue the men in peril. The helicopter races to the scene as you put on your wetsuit, get into your harness, and check the **rescue basket** one last time. When you reach the frantic fishermen, the helicopter hovers above the site, lowers you toward the water, and...Splash!

You dive into the choppy sea and start swimming. When you arrive at the lifeboat, you secure the first fisherman into the rescue basket and signal crewmates aboard the helicopter to hoist him aboard. You repeat this difficult process four more times before you hook up your own safety harness to be hauled back up into the helicopter—exhausted and happy about this good outcome.

Mission Accomplished

While the helicopter races back to the cutter, you provide blankets for the cold, wet fishermen and take their vital signs. Medical technicians on the cutter will take over to provide emergency medical treatment once you've landed.

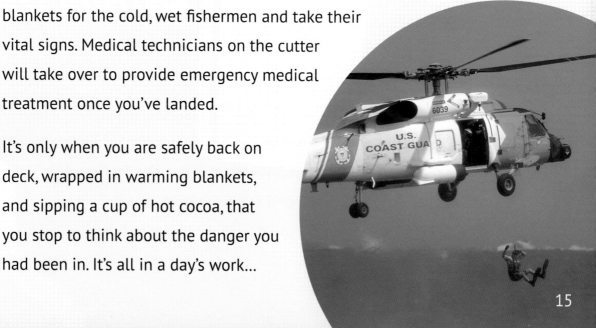

It's only when you are safely back on deck, wrapped in warming blankets, and sipping a cup of hot cocoa, that you stop to think about the danger you had been in. It's all in a day's work...

Your Coast Guard Rescue Swimmer Career Adventure Starts Here

EXPLORE IT!

Use your Internet research skills to find more about the following:

Amazing Coast Guard rescue stories

U.S. Coast Guard rescue swimmer videos on YouTube

Water safety tips

TRY IT!

Swim Like a Fish

Take swim lessons, join a community swimming team, and—when you are old enough—look into getting certified as a lifeguard through the YMCA. In other words, swim, swim, swim as much as you can! It's the only way to gain the superior skills needed to become a Coast Guard rescue swimmer.

First Aid Ready

Both the American Red Cross (www.redcross.org) and the American Heart Association (www.heart.org) offer first aid and CPR training for kids. Ask your parent or school PE teacher to help you find a local chapter and learn all you can about how to help out in emergency situations.

DEPUTY SECRETARY OF DEFENSE

Accomplished leader needed to help run one of the world's largest and most powerful military organizations. Will be responsible for millions of civilian and military employees and billions of dollars of taxpayer money. Must be trustworthy, decisive, and very smart. This is the ultimate Pentagon paper-pusher position!

- **Ready to take on this challenge?**
  Turn to page 18.

- **Want to explore a career as a Marine Raider instead?**
  Go to page 21.

- **Rather consider other choices?**
  Return to page 4.

Explore the Pentagon online at **www.history. com/topics/pentagon**.

Second in Charge

Let's start at the top. The president of the United States is the commander-in-chief of all five military branches. The president selects a secretary of defense to run the Department of Defense and its 2 million civilian and military employees. It's a big job and the secretary of defense needs help. So the president also appoints a **deputy secretary of defense**.

That's you—the second-highest ranking official in the Department of Defense of the United States of America. Fortunately, you are too busy managing the $500 billion defense budget to let all that power go to your head.

The Military Business

One of your main jobs is to run the business side of the military including making sure all that money is well-spent on the things the military needs to defend the nation. This includes everything from payroll to battleships. There are big decisions to make and many meetings to attend.

In addition to having military posts and bases around the country, the United States has a military presence in many nations around the world. One of your jobs is to make sure military resources are being used in the best ways possible to keep the world a safe and peaceful place. There is so much at stake and so many decisions to make. You have to get this right!

Right now your focus is on the Asia Pacific region. You are preparing to make a trip to Hawaii, Guam, South Korea, and Japan to talk strategy with military leaders. You might have thought you had lots of homework when you were in school. But studying for the toughest exam was nothing compared to what it takes to prepare for top level meetings like this. There are reports to read, briefings to attend, and information to analyze. People expect the deputy secretary of defense to know what he or she is talking about!

Smart Choices

Bottom line, lots of important people answer to you and lots of people want to be your friend. After all, you make decisions that can make or break huge business deals. Your choices can help or hinder international partnerships. You have to keep your wits about you at all times to make sure you are acting in your nation's best interests. Your work is all about protecting America and keeping the peace.

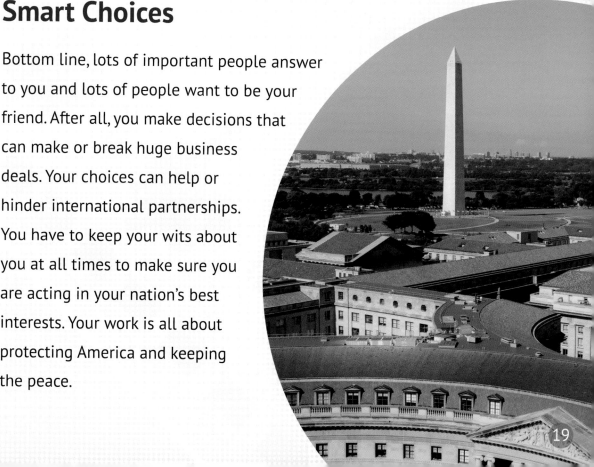

Your Deputy Secretary of Defense Career Adventure Starts Here

EXPLORE IT!

Use your Internet research skills to find more about the following:

Images of the Pentagon

History of the Pentagon

The secretary of defense and the president's cabinet

TRY IT!

About That Budget

The Department of Defense has an annual budget of around $500 billion. That's a lot of money to spend! What does that amount look like? Make up a list of all the things you could buy if you had just one million bucks. Now imagine you had to do that 500,000 times. That's how big the military budget is. Wow!

Where in the World is the U.S. Military?

Print out a map of the world and use markers to color in all the nations where the United States has a military presence. (You can find lists online by using the question "where in the world is the U.S. military" to search for information.) If you really were the deputy secretary of defense, you would visit many of these places and meet with their top military leaders. What are the top 10 places you would want to visit?

MARINE RAIDER

Take a virtual tour of the National Museum of the Marine Corps at **www. usmcmuseum.org.**

Marine Corps looking for a few men and women to win our nation's battles. Must survive and thrive in intense 12-week boot camp training. Readiness to be first to fight in battle and face down foes required. Ability to follow orders, maintain superior physical fitness, and work as a team are must-have qualities. Minimum requirements include being at least 17 years old, a high school graduate, and a U.S. citizen.

- *Ready to take on this challenge?*
  Turn to page 22.

- *Want to explore a career as a Navy Sonar Technician instead?*
  Go to page 25.

- *Rather consider other choices?*
  Return to page 4.

Booyah!

You are rough. You are tough. You are a U.S. Marine. To be more specific, you are a U.S. **Marine Raider.** The roughest of the rough. The toughest of the tough. You are part of an elite special forces unit that deploys around the world in rapid response to tense military situations.

Yes, like all Marines, you are a combat-ready warrior. But you are also a negotiator, teacher, advisor, and problem-solver. And, wow!, you are in amazing physical shape—an agile athlete—making you a formidable opponent in any circumstance.

Not just any Marine gets to be a Raider. The checklist of required skills and character traits is long. Besides being an experienced soldier, you must have integrity , intelligence, physical ability, adaptability, initiative, determination, dependability, teamwork, interpersonal skills, and stress tolerance.

Semper Fi!

Your special forces unit is named after the legendary Raiders who fought in World War II. Those brave men were part of the very first special operations forces and they conducted dangerous raids in the Asia-Pacific region. You are proud to continue their proud tradition.

Combat-Ready Diplomat

You are a sergeant and your 14-man special operations team is stationed at Camp Pendleton in California. Your duffel bag stays packed and you are always ready to go wherever your country needs you. Sometimes you are sent on missions where your team takes quick and even lethal actions to seize, destroy, or capture a hostile area. Other times you respond to terrorism with strong counterterrorism tactics.

This time you are being sent to provide training and assistance to the military of a foreign government. You speak their language and are able to work one-on-one with your foreign peers to teach them how to combat terrorists and keep their own nation secure.

Ready and Willing

As usual, this mission is top secret. You aren't even allowed to tell your family where you are. But this is your favorite type of mission, because it offers the best hope of bringing peace to an ally. And you are staying true to the Marine's motto: semper fidelis—always faithful.

Your Marine Raider Career Adventure Starts Here

EXPLORE IT!

Use your Internet research skills to find more about the following:

History of the World War II Marine Raiders

Famous Marines past and present

Semper fidelis, espirit de corps, and ductus exemplo

TRY IT!

Mini-Marine Boot Camp

If you are a boy, can you do three pull-ups, 50 sit-ups in two minutes, and run 3 miles (4.8 kilometers) in 28 minutes or less? If you are a girl, can you do a flex-arm hang for at least 15 seconds, 50 sit-ups in two minutes, and run 3 miles (4.8 kilometers) in 31 minutes or less? If not, it's time to get cracking! Marines must be in tip-top physical condition to make it out of boot camp.

Marine Timeline

The Marines have a proud tradition that began during the American Revolution and continues to this day. Go online to websites like www.marines.com/history-heritage/timeline to find out what the Marines have accomplished over the years. Make a timeline to record your favorite Marine moments in history.

NAVY SUBMARINE SONAR TECHNICIAN

Ready to live and work aboard a state-of-the-art submarine? Are you trustworthy, smart, and one of the best sailors in the U.S. Navy? High-tech sailor needed now! Must be able to process huge amounts of information, live in very close quarters, and perform well under pressure. Ability to keep secrets and be a team player required.

- **Ready to take on this challenge?**
  Turn to page 26.

- **Want to explore a career as an Air Force pilot instead?**
  Go to page 5.

- **Rather consider other choices?**
  Return to page 4.

Find out what's it like to work on a submarine at www.navy.com/navy-life/life-on-a-sub.html.

Reporting for Duty

As you prepare to board the *USS North Carolina,* you stop and take one last look at the Honolulu, Hawaii, shoreline. You are a **submarine sonar technician** and you may not see the light of day for several weeks or months, and you don't want to forget what it looks like!

For the past several months you have been on **shore duty** at Naval Station Pearl Harbor making repairs, training, and preparing for today. This is the day that you and 136 other sailors start **sea duty** aboard one of the U.S. Navy's most powerful tools: a **nuclear-powered submarine**.

Your destination? Most of the time, you will be submerged several hundred feet below the surface of the Pacific Ocean. Even though you have **top secret security clearance**, you cannot talk about your mission to your family and friends. Submarine missions are super secretive. Stealth, speed, and power are what submarines are all about.

Home, Sweet, Submarine

Your main job is to be the eyes and ears of the submarine using high-tech sonar, communications, and navigation systems. Sonar detects underwater sounds that tell you where other ships are and where they are heading. It's like you are an underwater spy!

Good thing you aren't **claustrophobic**! Your "home" onboard the sub consists of a space of about 15 feet (4.5 millimeters) where you sleep and store all your stuff. Your days will involve six hours of work, six hours of free time, and six hours of sleep. The only way you'll be able to tell night from day is by the food you eat. Pancakes mean breakfast. Beef stew means dinner.

Dive, Dive, Dive

You stow your gear and head for the submarine "nerve center." It isn't long before the submarine is far from land and you hear the captain give your favorite command over the intercom, "Submerge the ship!"

You hear the reply, "Aye, aye, sir. Dive." And so you begin what will be a journey of more than 36,000 nautical miles (66,672 kilometers). Before you return to your home port, you will make stops at ports in Japan, Korea, and Guam. You'll participate in international training exercises, and do your part to keep America safe.

Your Navy Submarine Sonar Technician Career Adventure Starts Here

EXPLORE IT!

Use your Internet research skills to find out more about the following:

World War II attack on Pearl Harbor

The USS North Carolina

How submarines work

TRY IT!

Submarines Then and Now

The *H.L. Hunley* was a famous Civil War submarine. It was the first submarine to successfully sink an enemy vessel. The *Hunley* later sank and was lost at sea for well over 100 years before it was recovered off the coast of Charleston, South Carolina. See what you can find out about the *Hunley* and compare it to modern submarines. Make a chart that compares and contrasts the features of past and present submarines.

Do-It-Yourself Submarine

Find instructions online for making a plastic bottle submarine. It's fun and it will give you a basic idea of how submarines work.

WRITE YOUR OWN CAREER ADVENTURE

WRITE YOUR OWN CAREER ADVENTURE

You just read about six awesome military careers:

- Air Force pilot
- Army cyber officer
- Coast Guard rescue swimmer
- Deputy secretary of defense
- Marine Raider
- Navy submarine sonar technician

Which is your favorite? Pick one, and imagine what it would be like to do that job. Now write your own career adventure!

_____

_____

_____

_____

_____

_____

_____

_____

Go online to download free activity sheets at www.cherrylakepublishing.com/activities.

ATTENTION, ADVENTURERS!
Please do NOT write in this book if it is not yours. Use a separate piece of paper.

GLOSSARY

aye a response that means yes

boots on the ground troops or soldiers who are on active service in a military operation on the ground

brigade a military unit having its own headquarters and consisting of two or more regiments, squadrons, groups, or battalions

claustrophobic suffering from an abnormal fear of being in enclosed or narrow places

commando soldier specially trained to carry out raids

CPR (cardiopulmonary resuscitation) an emergency lifesaving procedure

cutter light, fast coastal patrol boat

cyberattack attempt by hackers to damage or destroy a computer network or system

cyber officer person who protects computer networks and systems from cyberattacks

defensive intended to withstand, deter, or stop aggression or attack

deputy secretary of defense person who is number two in charge at the U.S. Department of Defense

Dolphin helicopter specially designed search-and-rescue helicopter operated by the U.S. Coast Guard

espionage ring group of spies used by governments to obtain political and military information

flight simulator machine designed to resemble the cockpit of an aircraft used for training pilots

formation formal arrangement of a number of persons or things acting as a unit, such as a troop of soldiers or aircraft in flight

Hurricane Katrina powerful hurricane that hit New Orleans and parts of the Gulf Coast in 2005

malicious intending or intended to do harm

Mayday international radio distress signal used by ships and aircraft

nuclear power form of energy produced by an atomic reaction

offensive making the first move to start a physical or military attack or assault

pilot person who flies military fighter jets or commercial airplanes

Raider elite fighting force within the Marines that responds to military situations around the world

rescue basket metal wire or plastic litter widely used to lift victims in search and rescue operations

rescue swimmer person who helps save those in trouble on the waters

sea duty naval service aboard a ship at sea

shore duty naval service performed at a home port

sonar method for locating objects and other vessels underwater by means of sound waves that are sent out and then reflected by the objects they encounter

submarine sonar technician person who works with the high-tech sonar, communications, and navigation systems on a submarine

sortie flight by a military aircraft or a group of military aircraft

stealth the act of proceeding with silence, secrecy, and caution

terrorist person who uses violence and threats to intimidate or coerce, especially for political purposes

top secret security clearance determination by the United States government that a person or company is eligible for access to secret information

wingman pilot whose aircraft is positioned behind and outside the leading aircraft in a formation

INDEX

ABOUT THE AUTHOR

Diane Lindsey Reeves is the author of lots of children's books. She has written several original PEANUTS stories (published by Regnery Kids and Sourcebooks). She is especially curious about what people do and likes to write books that get kids thinking about all the cool things they can be when they grow up. She lives in Cary, North Carolina, and her favorite thing to do is play with her grandkids—Conrad, Evan, Reid, and Hollis Grace.